T0182606

Matoaka
The True Story of Pocahontas

Ætatis suæ 21. Aº 1616.

Matoaks als Rebecka daughter to the mighty Prince
Powhatan Emperour of Attanoughkomouck als Virginia
converted and baptized in the Christian faith, and
Wife to the wor.ll Mr Tho: Rolff.

THIS EDITION
Editorial Management by Oriel Square
Produced for DK by WonderLab Group LLC
Jennifer Emmett, Erica Green, Kate Hale, *Founders*

Editor Maya Myers; **Photography Editor** Nicole DiMella; **Managing Editor** Rachel Houghton;
Designers Project Design Company; **Researcher** Michelle Harris;
Copy Editor Lori Merritt; **Indexer** Connie Binder; **Proofreader** Susan K. Hom;
Authenticity Reader Dr. Naomi R. Caldwell; **Series Reading Specialist** Dr. Jennifer Albro

First American Edition, 2024
Published in the United States by DK Publishing, a division of Penguin Random House LLC
1745 Broadway, 20th Floor, New York, NY 10019

A catalog record for this book is available from the Library of Congress.
HC ISBN: 978-0-7440-9452-7
PB ISBN: 978-0-7440-9451-0

DK books are available at special discounts when purchased in bulk for sales promotions, premiums, fund-raising,
or educational use. For details, contact:
DK Publishing Special Markets, 1745 Broadway, 20th Floor, New York, NY 10019
SpecialSales@dk.com

Printed and bound in China

The publisher would like to thank the following for their kind permission to reproduce their images:
a=above; c=center; b=below; l=left; r=right; t=top; b/g=background
Alamy Stock Photo: 2020 Images 28, Ian Goodrick 27, Tim Graham 29, North Wind Picture Archives 13, 19;
National Portrait Gallery, Smithsonian Institution: National Portrait Gallery, Smithsonian Institution;
transfer from the National Gallery of Art; gift of the A.W. Mellon Educational and Charitable Trust, 1942 1

All other images © Dorling Kindersley Limited
For more information see: www.dkimages.com

www.dk.com

This book was made with Forest
Stewardship Council™ certified
paper – one small step in DK's
commitment to a sustainable future.
Learn more at
www.dk.com/uk/information/sustainability

Publisher's note: Different words can be used for groups of people who are indigenous to a place. This series uses terms preferred by members of
the group being discussed.

Matoaka
The True Story of Pocahontas

Jillian Metchooyeah

illustrations by Nicole Nordstrom

Contents

Who Was Pocahontas?

You may have heard of Pocahontas [poe-kuh-HON-tus]. Maybe you have seen a movie about her. You may have seen pictures.

But who was Pocahontas really?

Pocahontas was a Powhatan [pow-uh-TAN] girl. The Powhatan Chiefdom was a group of Indigenous tribes that lived in the eastern part of what is now Virginia. Historians believe Pocahontas was born around 1596.

Pocahontas never wrote down her thoughts or feelings. What we know about her comes from written and oral histories. Historians put information from different sources together like a puzzle.

Oral Histories

Oral histories are told from one generation to the next. Many Indigenous groups choose certain people, like Elders, to share their oral histories.

Indigenous Names

Some Indigenous people have more than one name. Family members and community members can give names. The Powhatan people had different names throughout life.

When she was born, Pocahontas was named Amonute [ah-muh-NOO-tay]. Her personal name was Matoaka [mah-TOE-kuh]. It may have meant "flower between two streams."

Pocahontas was a nickname.
It may have meant "mischief"
or "laughing and joyous one."
She would have another name
later in her life. This book uses
her personal name, Matoaka.

Daughter of a Chief

The Powhatan called their homeland Tsenacomoco [TSEN-uh-ko-MAH-kuh]. Matoaka was around 11 years old when people from Europe first came to Tsenacomoco.

The Powhatan Chiefdom included around 30 tribes then. They were all ruled by Chief Powhatan. His personal name was Wahunsenaca [WAH-hun-SE-na-kuh].

Wahunsenaca was Matoaka's father. He was from the Pamunkey Tribe, the largest tribe in the Powhatan Chiefdom. Matoaka's mother was from the Mattaponi Tribe. Matoaka had many siblings.

In Matoaka's tribe, everyone worked. Women planted and harvested food. They gathered plants and fruit to eat.

Settlement at Jamestown

In 1607, a group of English people started a settlement at Tsenacomoco. They called it Jamestown. A trading company called the Virginia Company paid for the English people to go there. The company wanted to take control of the area. The company wanted to get wealthy.

One of the English people was John Smith. He was a soldier and an explorer. He made maps and wrote books.

Smith was caught by members of the Powhatan Chiefdom. They took him to the Powhatan capital, Werowocomoco [WHERE-oh-wo-ko-MO-ko]. He met with Chief Powhatan. Smith was released shortly after their meeting.

Matoaka and John Smith

In 1624, Smith wrote that Matoaka saved his life. His story has been retold for hundreds of years. But Smith was known for making up stories. Historians believe he made up this story. His life was never in danger. His story became a myth.

Matoaka and Smith did meet, however. Matoaka taught Smith some Algonquian [al-GON-kee-uhn], the language of the Powhatan. Smith taught Matoaka some English. Their friendship may have helped maintain peace among their people.

Symbol of Peace

Smith became the leader of Jamestown. Matoaka became an important person there. She acted as a translator. She helped the English and Powhatan communicate.

During the winter, the Powhatan sent gifts of food to Jamestown. They also traded.

Matoaka's father let her visit Jamestown as a sign of peace. Matoaka brought food to the settlement. She played with the children of Jamestown. They admired her amazing cartwheel skills.

Times of Tension

Peace between the Powhatan and the English did not last. Smith demanded more food than the Powhatan could give. He threatened to take their food. The Powhatan refused to be treated this way. They moved their villages away.

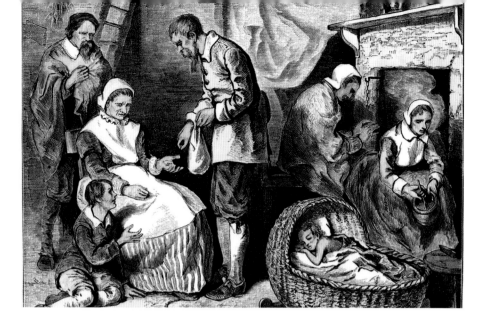

English people in Jamestown dividing their last kernels of corn

The English did not like Smith's strict leadership. They fought among themselves. Many English people starved. Smith returned to England.

Around this time, the oral histories say that Matoaka married an Indigenous man named Kocoum [KO-koo-um]. They had a child.

Kidnapped

In 1613, Matoaka was stolen from her family. The English took her to Jamestown. Her father was afraid she would be hurt if he tried to get her back.

Soon, she was moved to another settlement called Henrico [hen-RYE-koh].

In Henrico, she met an explorer named John Rolfe. He came on a ship with the Virginia Company. He was also a farmer. He wanted to grow tobacco.

Matoaka was baptized as a Christian. She was given a Christian name: Rebecca.

A Different Way of Life

Matoaka married Rolfe in 1614. The oral histories say that Matoaka married Rolfe to help make peace between the Powhatan and the English. Her father gave her a pearl necklace as a wedding gift.

Matoaka had a son named Thomas around this time.

Matoaka lived an English way of life, away from her people. Many of the customs and traditions from Matoaka's family and community were not part of this life.

Matoaka and other Powhatan people taught Rolfe a better way to dry tobacco. Selling this tobacco made him wealthy. The Virginia Company also became wealthy.

A Journey and an End

In 1616, Matoaka, Thomas, Rolfe, and a small group of Powhatan people visited England. Matoaka and the Powhatan wanted to learn things about the English. They hoped this would help their people back home.

In England, Matoaka met John Smith again. She was angry at him. He had disrespected her people and taken their land.

In 1617, Matoaka and her family decided to return to Virginia. However, Matoaka got sick on the trip. Before they arrived, she died. She was around 21 years old.

The oral histories say that
Matoaka suddenly became
ill after eating a meal. Some
people believe she was
poisoned. Some written
histories say other people
on the ship also became ill.

Matoaka's Legacy

We do not know the full story of Matoaka's life. But we know that she was taken from her family. Her story shows the difficult situations Indigenous peoples faced during her lifetime. Many Indigenous people continue to face hardships today. This is especially true for women and girls, just as it was for Matoaka.

Matoaka's story is also one of strength. She showed bravery and resilience when her life was difficult.

A monument at St. George's Church in Gravesend, England, where Matoaka was buried

Still Here

In 2015, the Pamunkey Tribe gained federal recognition. This allows a tribe to make its own laws. Some other tribes in Virginia are also federally recognized. Other tribes are working on gaining federal recognition.

In 1677, the Pamunkey and Mattaponi Tribes signed the Treaty of Middle Plantation. It said the tribes would keep rights to their lands. They would be protected. The tribes would present a tribute instead of paying taxes. The tribes still give a tribute of fresh food to the governor of Virginia each November.

Glossary

Baptize
A Christian ceremony that makes a person a member of the church

Christian
A person who believes in and/or was baptized in the Christian religion

Elder
An individual recognized by their community for their experience and knowledge of Indigenous traditions, who offers the community guidance and teachings based on their experience and knowledge

Explorer
A person who travels to an area that is not known to them

Federal
A government that unites multiple states under a central government

Hardship
Something that is hard or difficult to experience

Historian
A person who studies and writes about the past

Indigenous people
The earliest known inhabitants of an area

Myth
A story told over many years that seems true but is not

Oral histories
A method of recording history by word of mouth. Oral histories gather, preserve, and interpret the voices and memories of people, communities, and events from the past.

Resilience
Ability to adjust to or recover from difficult situations

Settlement
A place where people have recently set up homes

Sibling
A relative who shares at least one parent with another person

Taxes
Money paid to a government, used to pay for government services

Translator
A person who changes words from one language to words that mean the same thing in another language

Treaty
A formal agreement among groups of people

Tribe (Indigenous)
A group or community of Indigenous people. Different Indigenous groups may use different terms, such as nation, clan, or band, to refer to themselves.

Index

Quiz

Answer the questions to see what you have learned. Check your answers in the key below.

1. What were three other names given to Matoaka throughout her life?

2. True or false: Matoaka taught John Smith the Algonquian language.

3. About how many tribes made up the Powhatan Chiefdom?

4. True or false: Matoaka acted as a translator between the Powhatans and the English.

5. What year did the Pamunkey Tribe gain federal recognition?

1. Amonute, Pocahontas, and Rebecca 2. True 3. 30
4. True 5. 2015